Ping & Pong

based on the poem by
Dennis Lee

adapted and illustrated by
David McPhail

AN ALLIGATOR PRESS BOOK

▟▙ HarperCollins*Publishers*Ltd

At Home:
The Joys Of Child-Rearing

Then, One Day At Lunch ...

Peter And Patrick Still Had Their Differences...
All Friends Do.

But They Didn't Fight Any More.

Amazing Things. They Travelled Far And Wide.

Their Whole Lives Through.

Peter Ping and Patrick Pong

When Peter Ping met Patrick Pong
They stared like anything.
For Ping (in fact) looked more like Pong,
While Pong looked more like Ping.

The reason was, a nurse had changed
Their cribs, and got them wrong—
So no one knew, their whole lives through,
That Pong was Ping; Ping, Pong.

David McPhail writes:

The first time I read Dennis Lee's evocative poem "Ping and Pong"
I knew there was more to the story, and I felt compelled to tell it.
This book is the result.
Others may read the poem and interpret it in an entirely different
way — that's fine — but this is my book, and this is how I see it.

Dennis Lee writes:

It's true that I wrote "Ping and Pong." But I didn't understand
my own poem. I thought it was about a logical impossibility,
in which one person "looks more like another," and vice versa.
What a shallow reading that was! Now that David McPhail has
uncovered the real story of Ping and Pong, I'm amazed.
I never knew.

Produced by Caterpillar Press for
HarperCollins Publishers Ltd
Suite 2900, Hazelton Lanes
55 Avenue Road
Toronto, Ontario M5R 3L2 Canada

93 94 95 96 97 98 99   First Edition   10 9 8 7 6 5 4 3 2 1

Canadian Cataloguing in Publication Data
Lee, Dennis, 1939 -
Ping and Pong

ISBN 0-00-223996-5

I McPhail, David, 1940 - .II. Title
PS8523.E44P56 1993   jC811'.54   C93-093630-2
PZ8.3.L44Pi 1993

"Blame David."
–Dennis Lee